PENGUIN BOOKS

Country Women's Association
Biscuits and Slices

Country Women's Association

Biscuits and Slices

TRADITIONAL, TEMPTING, TRIED-AND-TRUE

PENGUIN BOOKS

Contents

Foreword

The Country Women's Association of Australia has been in existence for more than 80 years and its members have long had a reputation for being wonderful cooks. Indeed, too often it seems that the public and the media think that our main activity is 'making tea and scones', though this is far from the case. But it is true that cooking and catering by our members, especially at local agricultural shows, have always been a major source of fundraising, enabling the CWA to raise many hundreds of thousands of dollars over the years, which has been used to support families and communities particularly in rural areas.

The recipes in this series of cookbooks reflect the way in which our pioneer women used the simple ingredients they had to hand to make nutritious snacks, soups, stews, sweets and cakes, and would ensure their household a year-round supply of jams, jellies and relishes by preserving fruit when it was in season. Some of these recipes are family favourites and have been handed down through the generations, being adapted along the way to suit the available ingredients and local conditions. Many members have also adopted and adapted 'new' foods introduced to Australia from other countries.

We are proud to be working with Penguin Books in pulling together these cookbooks and to be sharing with you our members' prized recipes. In so doing, once again CWA members are providing a valuable service to rural communities, as the royalties from the series (and from the recipe book *Country Classics*, which was republished by Penguin in 2007) will help us fund a postgraduate nursing scholarship. This is awarded to a nurse working in a rural area, allowing them to learn new skills and thus continue to provide an essential service to their community.

The scholarship is of especial importance as we see the nation's health services struggling – in all parts of Australia, but particularly in rural communities where sometimes the nurse is the only health professional available.

May you get as much pleasure from trying these recipes as the members of the Country Women's Association have in sharing them with you.

Lesley Young
National President (2006–2009)
Country Women's Association of Australia

About the CWA

The Country Women's Association was established in Australia during the early 1920s, in New South Wales. A conference was organised in Sydney in 1922 to coincide with the Easter Show, a time when many rural women 'came to town' with their families. There were increasing shared concerns about the issues facing women and their families in rural communities, and as well as agreeing on various social and political objectives the conference saw a committee formed to establish an organisation to promote the interests of women on the land. The idea was not new, as rural women's organisations had been around for many years in other parts of the world, the first recorded group having been formed in Finland in the 1700s.

Following the formation of this first CWA branch, many more spread throughout New South Wales and in other states. By the late 1930s there were CWA offices in all states and territories of Australia. During World War II the associations contributed in a number of ways to the war effort: local branches made their rooms and other facilities available and produced food, entertainment, equipment and clothing for Australian servicemen. They also helped the many women who were left behind to run the family farm while their husbands were away at the war.

In 1945 the state associations agreed to form a national body, the Country Women's Association of Australia. The first national meeting was held in Adelaide in 1946. Since those early days, our members have continued to support rural families and have lobbied governments on all sorts of matters including education, health, transport, aged care, child care and libraries. They have also addressed broader issues such as commodity prices, farm safety, GM crops, and water.

We are part of a world organisation of more than 9 million members in about 70 countries, the Associated Country Women of the World. The funds raised from our 'tea and scones' and other enterprises have allowed us to support many people in many different ways, not just in the country but throughout Australia and also overseas, including our sister members in the South Pacific.

At home, the range and scope of our activities have been of particular importance during the recent drought years, with money being donated from all levels of government and from corporations such as Woolworths (through their 'Drought Days' program), Bega Cheese and many others, for us to distribute to affected families. We have been able to pay families' emergency household expenses, have held community get-togethers, and have also supported other rural organisations. In addition to drought, some areas have experienced extreme and devastating rains and bushfires, and our branches have been able to assist, from their own emergency funds, those suffering hardship as a result.

Today we have some 44000 members in 1855 branches country-wide. Even though our membership numbers are dwindling, I am confident that the Country Women's Association of Australia will continue to support rural communities for at least another 80 years. If you are interested in helping us with this work, we encourage you to join up – there will be a branch near you. Give your state office a call and see how you can become part of an organisation that cares for families not only in rural and remote areas but throughout Australia.

Biscuits

Foundation biscuit recipe

My mother used to make the cinnamon version of this recipe often.

PATRICIA WALKER, GEORGE TOWN BRANCH, TAS.

1½ cups plain flour

1 tablespoon cornflour

1 teaspoon baking powder

pinch of salt

115 g softened butter

½ cup sugar

1 x 50-g egg, lightly beaten

MAKES ABOUT 40

Preheat the oven to 190°C. Grease baking trays.

Sift together flours, baking powder and salt. In a separate bowl, cream butter and sugar very well. Gradually beat in egg until mixture is creamy. Work in the flour mixture to make a fairly stiff dough. Divide dough into three portions and roll each piece into a log 3 cm in diameter. Using a wet knife, cut the logs into slices. Roll each slice into a ball, place on prepared trays and press with the back of a wet fork. Bake for 10–15 minutes, until pale golden-brown. Cool well on the trays before storing.

Variations

Lemon biscuits: Add grated zest of 1 lemon to the mixture (with the butter). Decorate each biscuit with a small piece of candied orange peel.

Raspberry roll: Roll out dough until quite thin, then spread thinly with jam and roll up. Cut into slices 5 mm thick, then coat with desiccated coconut.

Cinnamon biscuits: Add 1 tablespoon ground cinnamon to the mixture (with the flour).

Five dozen biscuits

This recipe is so-named because five dozen is about how many biscuits it makes. You can use this dough to make all kinds of biscuits – really, the variations are limited only by your imagination.

MARIAN MUDRA, KUMBIA BRANCH, QLD

500 g butter or cooking margarine
12 tablespoons sugar
1 × 395-g can condensed milk
4–5 cups self-raising flour

MAKES 5 DOZEN

Preheat the oven to 190°C. Grease baking trays.

Mix all ingredients together, adding enough sifted flour to give a nice workable dough. Roll spoonfuls of dough into balls, place on prepared trays and flatten with the back of a fork. (Alternatively, you can roll the mixture into a sausage 2.5–3 cm in diameter, then cut into slices 5–10 mm thick.) Bake for 15–20 minutes, until crisp.

Variations
Assorted biscuits: Divide the dough into portions and add a different ingredient to each: desiccated coconut, chocolate chips, nuts, sultanas, cocoa.

Jam drops: Place balls of dough on trays, flatten slightly and use your finger or a wooden spoon to make an indent in the centre. Fill indent with jam.

Corn flakes biscuits: Roll the balls of dough in corn flakes before baking.

Coconut biscuits: Roll the balls of dough in desiccated coconut before baking.

Standard biscuit recipe

This is my most-used biscuit recipe. I've made hundreds of dozens of these biscuits in various shapes for Halloween, Christmas, Easter, Australia Day, Melbourne Cup, St Patrick's Day, Mothers' and Fathers' Day, as well as for weddings and department stores. My children and grandchildren make them each year for their teachers, school fêtes, etc. They can be packaged in tins, cellophane bags or jars for gifts.

JEAN F. MILES, CWA POTTERS BRANCH, VIC.

110 g softened butter
½ cup caster sugar
1 egg
½ teaspoon vanilla essence
¾ cup plain flour
¾ cup self-raising flour

MAKES ABOUT 50

Preheat the oven to 160°C. Grease baking trays.

Cream butter and sugar, then beat in egg and vanilla. Add sifted flours and mix to a dough. Roll out the dough, then cut out shapes with biscuit cutters. Place on prepared trays. Bake for 8–10 minutes.

Variations
A base for slices (e.g. marshmallow slice, caramel slice, peppermint slice): Roll out the dough and use to line a slice tin, then spread with desired topping. Bake at 180°C for 15–20 minutes.

Fruit flan: Roll out the dough on a sheet of cling wrap, then invert onto a pizza tray, remove plastic and trim edges. Bake at 180°C for about 20 minutes. When cold, arrange drained canned fruit or fresh fruit (like strawberries) over the flan base. Make a clear glaze to brush over the fruit, or purchase a packet of glaze from any good delicatessen. (The base can be cooked in advance and stored in an airtight container, or else frozen, until you require it.)

Date roll: Roll out the dough and cut into small rectangular pieces, then roll a date inside each (like a sausage roll). Brush with melted butter and sprinkle with caster sugar. Bake at 180°C for 8–10 minutes.

Decorated biscuits: Roll a teaspoon of the biscuit mixture into a ball and coat with coffee crystals, Hundreds and Thousands or sprinkles, caster sugar or spices, or push a nut or cherry into the top. Bake at 180°C for 8–10 minutes.

Filled biscuits: Join cooked biscuits with jam or icing.

Flavoured biscuits: Add 2 tablespoons caraway seeds, a few chopped nuts or some mixed fruit to the mixture. Roll into balls, place on a baking tray and flatten with the back of a fork before baking. For chocolate biscuits, add a tablespoon of cocoa after the egg has been beaten in. Bake at 180°C for 8–10 minutes.

Easter bunnys: Roll a small ball of dough for the head and a slightly larger one for the body, then roll ears, and put on currant eyes and a cherry mouth, or ice the face when cold (or to make 'backwards' bunnies, leave the head plain and roll a small ball of dough for a tail). Bake at 180°C for 8–10 minutes.

Whatever biscuits

MRS. KATHY FRANKCOMBE, SHEFFIELD BRANCH, TAS.

110 g softened butter

½ cup sugar

1 egg

1 cup self-raising flour

1 cup of 'whatever' (sultanas,
 choc chips, muesli, corn flakes,
 chopped unsalted peanuts,
 chopped dried apricots, etc.)

MAKES ABOUT 20

Preheat the oven to 180°C. Grease baking trays.

Cream butter and sugar, then add egg and beat well.
Add sifted flour and the 'whatever' ingredient and mix.
Roll mixture into balls the size of a walnut, place on pre-
pared trays and bake for 10–15 minutes.

Monte Carlos

JOYCE GOOS, VALENTINE PLAINS BRANCH, QLD

120 g softened butter

½ cup sugar

1 egg

1 tablespoon honey

1¼ cups self-raising flour

1¼ cups plain flour

jam, for joining

icing

1 cup icing sugar

2 teaspoons butter

MAKES 30–34

Preheat the oven to 180°C. Grease baking trays.

Cream butter and sugar. Beat in egg and honey. Sift in flours and mix well. Roll mixture into balls, place on prepared baking trays and flatten with the back of a fork. Bake for 10–15 minutes. Set aside to cool.

Make icing by combining sifted icing sugar with butter and just enough warm water to make a spreading consistency.

Join cooled biscuits together with jam and icing.

Corn flakes cakes

I learnt to make these biscuits in cookery class at state school back in 1945. I also learnt jam drops but in those days they were named pansy faces.

MARY HANSLOW, ORIELTON BRANCH, TAS.

110 g softened butter

½ cup sugar

1 egg

170 g self-raising flour

¼ teaspoon salt

2 heaped tablespoons sultanas

corn flakes, to coat

MAKES 24–30

Preheat the oven to 180°C. Chill a baking tray.

Cream butter and sugar, then add egg and beat well. Mix in sifted flour and salt, and stir in sultanas. Roll teaspoonfuls of mixture into balls, then roll in the corn flakes, to coat. Put balls on the cold oven tray and bake for about 15 minutes, until golden-brown.

Ginger crispies

PHYLLIS HINGSTON, SASSAFRAS/WESLEY VALE BRANCH, TAS.

500 g softened butter

500 g sugar

1 egg, beaten

1²/₃ cups self-raising flour

1 cup chopped sweet preserved ginger

cornflour, to coat

MAKES 25–30

Preheat the oven to 180°C. Grease a baking tray.

Cream butter and sugar, then beat in egg and lastly add sifted flour and ginger. Mix well. Form mixture into small balls and roll in cornflour to coat. Place on prepared tray and bake for 10 minutes.

Greek Easter biscuits

JUDY ANICTOMATIS, DARWIN BRANCH, NT

250 g softened unsalted butter

1½ cups sugar

3 tablespoons vanillin sugar

4 eggs, plus 1 extra for glazing

½ glass orange juice

½ glass milk

¼ teaspoon salt

grated zest of 3 oranges (orange part only)

1½ teaspoons baking powder

about 1 kg self-raising flour

sesame seeds, for sprinkling

MAKES 60–70

Preheat the oven to 170°C. Line baking trays with baking paper.

Cream butter and sugar, then add vanillin sugar, eggs, orange juice, milk, salt and orange zest. Beat well. Add baking powder and enough sifted flour to achieve a good dough consistency – keep adding flour until mixture is smooth and workable. Roll dough into long snakes, then form into plaits about 8 cm long. Alternatively, you can roll a snake 25 cm long, then fold it in half, twist it, and join ends together to form a circle. (These are just two of the shapes traditionally made at Easter time.)

Put shapes on prepared baking trays, brush with beaten egg and sprinkle with the sesame seeds. Bake for 15–20 minutes until golden-brown.

Quick and easy biscuits

P. SAUNDERS, SELBOURNE BRANCH, TAS.

2 cups self-raising flour

1 cup soft brown sugar

2 cups dried fruit (dates, raisins, etc.)

230 g butter, melted

MAKES 24

Preheat the oven to 180°C. Line a scone tray with baking paper.

Mix sifted flour with sugar and fruit. Pour melted butter slowly over the dry ingredients, stirring continually. Spread mixture over the prepared tray and cook for 20 minutes. Cut into squares while hot, then allow to cool on the tray. Store in an airtight container once cold.

Ginger creams

MARY HANSLOW, ORIELTON BRANCH, TAS.

230 g softened butter

1 cup sugar

1 tablespoon golden syrup

1 egg, beaten

2½ cups plain flour

1 teaspoon bicarbonate of soda

1 level tablespoon ground ginger

filling

1 cup icing sugar

1 tablespoon melted butter

vanilla essence, to taste

pink food colouring (optional)

2–3 teaspoons hot water

MAKES 60

Preheat the oven to 180°C. Grease baking trays.

Cream butter and sugar, then beat in golden syrup and egg. Sift together flour, soda and ginger, add to the creamed mixture and mix well. Roll out the dough and cut out shapes, or use a biscuit forcer. Place on prepared trays and bake for about 10 minutes, until golden-brown.

To make the icing, combine sifted icing sugar with butter, vanilla to taste, a few drops of food colouring (if using) and enough hot water to make a spreading consistency.

Sandwich biscuits together with icing when cold.

Jelly crystal biscuits

BERRIS SHARMAN, SPREYTON BRANCH, TAS.

225 g softened butter

2 × 85-g packets jelly crystals

2 eggs, beaten

3 small cups self-raising flour

1 tablespoon cornflour

white sugar, to coat

MAKES 36

Preheat the oven to 180°C. Grease a baking tray.

Cream butter and jelly crystals, beat in eggs, then add sifted flours. Roll mixture into balls then toss them in sugar to coat. Place on prepared baking tray and press with the back of a fork. Bake for 15–20 minutes, until golden-brown.

Ginger biscuits

JOYCE GOOS, VALENTINE PLAINS BRANCH, QLD

2 tablespoons softened butter

¾ cup sugar

1 egg

3 dessertspoons treacle

2 cups plain flour

1 teaspoon bicarbonate of soda

1 teaspoon ground cinnamon

1 teaspoon ground ginger

1 teaspoon mixed spice

MAKES 30

Preheat the oven to 180°C. Grease baking trays.

Cream butter and sugar, then beat in egg and treacle. Sift in flour, bicarb soda and spices and mix well. Roll mixture into balls, place on prepared baking trays and flatten with a fork. Bake for 15–20 minutes.

Butterscotch cookies

ANITA MORRISH, VICTORIA HILL BRANCH, QLD

120 g softened butter
1 cup soft brown sugar
pinch of salt
vanilla essence, to taste
1 egg
1½ cups self-raising flour
½ cup rice bubbles

MAKES 24–30

Preheat the oven to 180°C. Grease baking trays.

Cream butter and sugar, then beat in salt, vanilla and egg. Sift in flour, add rice bubbles and mix. Knead until dough is smooth. If you're in a hurry, just place spoonfuls onto prepared trays and press with the back of a fork. Otherwise, roll mixture into a log, wrap in greased paper and chill until firm, then cut into slices and place onto trays. Bake until golden-brown.

Luncheon biscuits

PHYLLIS HINGSTON, SASSAFRAS/WESLEY VALE BRANCH, TAS.

2 tablespoons softened butter

½ cup sugar

1 egg, well beaten

1 cup sultanas

vanilla essence, to taste

1 cup self-raising flour

pinch of salt

MAKES 24–30

Preheat the oven to 180°C. Grease a baking tray.

Cream butter and sugar. Beat in egg, then mix in sultanas, vanilla and sifted flour and salt. Place heaped teaspoons of mixture on prepared tray. Cook for 10–15 minutes, until golden-brown.

Macaroons

My mother, Euphemia Matheson, always had a tin of these biscuits for after-school snacks.

AILSA BOND A.M., RIVERSIDE BRANCH, TAS.

230 g softened butter
230 g sugar
340 g plain flour
1 teaspoon baking powder
1 teaspoon vanilla essence
2 eggs
almonds, for decorating

MAKES 24

Preheat the oven to 180°C. Grease baking trays.

Cream butter and sugar, then add all other ingredients and mix well. Make dough into small balls, place on prepared trays and put an almond on top of each. Bake for 10–15 minutes.

Apricot candy balls

JOYCE GOOS, VALENTINE PLAINS BRANCH, QLD

1½ cups chopped dried apricots
2½ cups desiccated coconut
¾ cup condensed milk
icing sugar, to coat

MAKES 30–34

Mix together the apricots, coconut and condensed milk. Roll mixture into small balls, then toss in icing sugar to coat. Allow to dry before serving.

Annie's biscuits

MARY HANSLOW, ORIELTON BRANCH, TAS.

55 g softened butter

¼ cup sugar

1 egg

1 large dessertspoon cornflour

1 cup self-raising flour

MAKES 20

Preheat the oven to 180°C. Grease a baking tray.

Cream butter and sugar, then beat in egg. Add sifted flours and mix well. Roll out the dough and cut into shapes or use a biscuit forcer. Place on prepared tray and bake for about 10 minutes.

Tyne's shortbread

This recipe came from Reece High School in Devonport, Tasmania. My granddaughter made it at school and I think it is the best shortbread I have ever made. I like to add some vanilla. (I never had any method given to me, so here is how I make it.)

BETTY LEHMAN, SPREYTON BRANCH, TAS.

¾ cup icing sugar

250 g softened butter

1 teaspoon vanilla essence

2½ cups plain flour

almonds or glacé cherries,
   for decorating

MAKES ABOUT 36

Preheat the oven to 160°C. Grease baking trays.

Cream the sifted icing sugar with the butter, then add vanilla. Sift in the flour, then knead a little. Roll dough into small balls, place on prepared trays and flatten with the back of a fork. Top with an almond or a piece of glacé cherry. Bake for 10–15 minutes until you are happy with the colour, but do not brown.

Shortbread

AILSA BOND A.M., RIVERSIDE BRANCH, TAS.

285 g plain flour
2/3 cup icing sugar
230 g butter

MAKES ABOUT 25-30

Preheat the oven to 180°C. Grease a baking tray.

Mix the sifted flour and icing sugar with the butter until well combined. Roll dough into a long sausage shape. Put into the fridge to firm, then cut into slices. Place slices on prepared tray and cook for about 30 minutes. (Do not allow to brown.)

Rolled oat shortbread

PHYLLIS HINGSTON, SASSAFRAS/WESLEY VALE BRANCH, TAS.

125 g butter, melted

125 g sugar

125 g rolled oats

125 g desiccated coconut

MAKES 20–25

Preheat the oven to 180°C. Grease a Swiss roll tin.

Mix all ingredients together and put into prepared tin. Cook for 30 minutes. Cut into squares.

Greek shortbread (kourabiethes)

In this recipe I've described the way I make these biscuits, as this is how I learned to do so from the Greek ladies in our community some 40 years ago when I first got married. They didn't have recipe books or written recipes, so I went along to their houses and just wrote down how they made the sweets and biscuits. I've made some changes to suit myself.

JUDY ANICTOMATIS, DARWIN BRANCH, NT

500 g softened butter

6 tablespoons icing sugar, plus extra for dusting

500 g plain flour

500 g self-raising flour

1 good tablespoon brandy

1 tablespoon vanillin sugar

1 cup chopped toasted almonds

MAKES ABOUT 30

Preheat the oven to 150°C. Line baking trays with baking paper.

Cream butter and sifted icing sugar. Add 2 tablespoons of the plain flour and 2 tablespoons of the self-raising flour and mix. Add brandy, vanillin sugar and chopped almonds. Continue to gradually add equal parts of plain and self-raising flour, until the mixture is the right consistency for rolling out and cutting with cookie cutters (so the shapes don't fall apart). Roll out the dough and cut out shapes. Place onto trays and bake for 15–20 minutes or until light-brown. Allow to cool, then dust with icing sugar and store in an airtight container.

Apricot biscuits

MARY HANSLOW, ORIELTON BRANCH, TAS.

85 g softened butter

85 g sugar

1 tablespoon apricot jam

140 g self-raising flour

MAKES 20

Preheat the oven to 175°C. Grease a baking tray.

Cream butter and sugar, beat in jam then add sifted flour and mix well. Take small portions of the mixture and roll into balls. Place on prepared tray and press balls lightly with the back of a fork. Bake for 10–15 minutes, until golden-brown.

Coconut biscuits

ANITA MORRISH, VICTORIA HILL BRANCH, QLD

60 g softened butter

1 cup sugar

1 egg

pinch of salt

vanilla essence, to taste

1 cup desiccated coconut,
   plus extra for sprinkling

1½ cups self-raising flour

chocolate icing (page 179)

MAKES 20

Preheat oven to 180°C. Grease baking trays.

Cream butter and sugar, then beat in egg, salt and vanilla. Add coconut and sifted flour and mix well. Roll into balls, flatten a little with your hands and place on prepared trays. Bake for 20 minutes until golden-brown. Ice with chocolate icing and sprinkle with coconut.

Yo-yo biscuits

AILSA BOND A.M., RIVERSIDE BRANCH, TAS.

170 g softened butter

1/3 cup icing sugar

55 g custard powder

170 g plain flour

icing

2 tablespoons icing sugar

1 tablespoon softened butter

1/2 teaspoon vanilla essence

MAKES 24

Preheat the oven to 180°C. Grease a baking tray.

To make the biscuit dough, cream butter and icing sugar together. Add custard powder and well-sifted flour and mix well. Roll mixture into little balls, place on prepared trays and press down with the back of a fork. Bake for about 20 minutes.

To make the icing, combine sifted icing sugar with butter and vanilla essence until smooth.

When biscuits are cool, join together with the icing.

Refrigerator biscuits

MRS. KATHY FRANKCOMBE, SHEFFIELD BRANCH, TAS.

1²/₃ cups plain flour

½ teaspoon baking powder

¼ teaspoon salt

1 teaspoon mixed spice

170 g softened butter

1 cup firmly packed soft
   brown sugar

1 egg

1 teaspoon vanilla essence

110 g chopped walnuts

MAKES ABOUT 26

Preheat the oven to 180°C. Grease baking trays.

Sift together flour, baking powder, salt and spice. In a separate bowl cream butter and sugar well, then beat in egg and vanilla essence. Add dry ingredients to creamed mixture and mix well. Stir in chopped walnuts. Shape mixture into long logs about 4 cm in diameter. Cover with cling wrap and chill until firm.

Slice the logs into rounds and place on prepared baking trays. Bake for 7–10 minutes.

(Note: dough can be kept in the fridge for up to 2 weeks or frozen for a few months.)

Raisin snaps

These are war-time biscuits.

ANITA MORRISH, VICTORIA HILL BRANCH, QLD

240 g softened butter

1½ cups sugar

pinch of salt

vanilla essence, to taste

2 tablespoons golden syrup

4 eggs

3 cups self-raising flour

½ teaspoon ground cinnamon

1 teaspoon bicarbonate of soda

1 cup raisins, plus extra for
  decorating

MAKES ABOUT 50

Preheat the oven to 180°C. Grease baking trays.

Cream butter and sugar. Beat in salt, vanilla, golden syrup and eggs. Add sifted flour, cinnamon and bicarb soda and mix. Stir in raisins. Drop teaspoonfuls of mixture onto prepared trays and press with the back of a fork. Place a raisin on top of each and cook for 10 minutes, until golden-brown.

Ginger balls

JOYCE GOOS, VALENTINE PLAINS BRANCH, QLD

1 × 250-g packet Ginger Nut biscuits, crushed

1 × 395-g can condensed milk

1 cup desiccated coconut, plus extra to coat

1 × 125-g packet crystallised ginger, chopped

MAKES 30–34

Mix together the crushed biscuits, condensed milk, coconut and crystallised ginger. Roll into balls and toss in coconut to coat. Refrigerate until set.

Choc-cream biscuits

MARY HANSLOW, ORIELTON BRANCH, TAS.

85 g softened butter

½ cup sugar

1 teaspoon vanilla essence

1 egg yolk

¾ cup self-raising flour

1 tablespoon cornflour

2 tablespoons cocoa

filling

2 tablespoons butter

½ cup icing sugar

3 tablespoons powdered milk

vanilla essence, to taste

MAKES 16

Preheat the oven to 180°C. Grease a baking tray.

Cream butter and sugar, then add vanilla and egg yolk and beat well. Sift in flours and cocoa and mix well. Roll teaspoonfuls of mixture into balls, place on prepared tray and flatten with the back of a fork. Cook in the oven for about 15 minutes, until set.

To make the filling, put butter in a small saucepan and place over a saucepan of boiling water until melted. Add sifted icing sugar and milk powder, and vanilla essence to taste and mix well.

When biscuits are cold, ice together with the filling.

Chocolate biscuits

WILMA DELL, DEVONPORT BRANCH, TAS.

125 g cooking chocolate, chopped
125 g softened butter
2 tablespoons sugar
2 tablespoons condensed milk
1 cup self-raising flour

MAKES 30

Preheat the oven to 180°C. Grease a baking tray.

Melt cooking chocolate in a heatproof bowl set over a pan of simmering water (or in the microwave). In a separate bowl, cream butter and sugar, then add condensed milk, melted chocolate and finally the sifted flour. Put small balls of mixture on prepared tray, and press each with the back of a fork. (For fancier biscuits, mark with the fork once, then turn fork ninety degrees and mark again.) Bake for 15–20 minutes.

Chocolate chip biscuits

I make these biscuits with my friend's children. They love to help me cook. Decorating the biscuits with choc chips is a great job for children, although I have to say that more choc chips get eaten than used! (You can use any type of choc chips you like for this recipe, or use chopped chocolate or even nuts instead.)

MELISSA ANICTOMATIS, PORT DARWIN BRANCH, NT

150 g softened unsalted butter

¼ cup soft brown sugar

⅓ cup caster sugar

1 egg yolk

1 teaspoon vanilla extract

1½ cups self-raising flour

½ cup dark chocolate chips

½ cup milk chocolate chips

MAKES 24

Preheat oven to 180°C. Grease and line a baking tray.

Beat the butter, sugars and egg yolk together until light and creamy. Add the vanilla and beat until combined. Sift in the flour and add ¼ cup of each type of choc chips. Fold in using a metal spoon, until just combined. Use your hands to push the mixture together to form a soft dough. Roll level tablespoons of the mixture into balls and place on prepared tray (allow room for spreading during cooking). Slightly flatten the balls then press remaining choc chips on top. Bake for 15 minutes or until crisp and lightly browned.

Choc-apricot cookies

MARY HANSLOW, ORIELTON BRANCH, TAS.

125 g softened butter

⅓ cup caster sugar

½ cup firmly packed soft
 brown sugar

1 egg, lightly beaten

1 cup self-raising flour

1 cup chocolate chips

1 cup shredded coconut

¾ cup chopped dried apricots

MAKES 30

Preheat the oven to 180°C. Grease a baking tray.

Cream butter and sugars until light and fluffy. Beat in egg until just combined. Stir in sifted flour, choc chips, coconut and apricots. Mix to a firm dough.

Place teaspoonfuls of mixture onto prepared tray, spaced about 5 cm apart, and flatten slightly. Bake for about 15 minutes. Remove from the oven and let stand on the tray for 5 minutes before turning onto a wire rack to cool.

Anzac biscuits

Traditionally, these biscuits have been sent overseas to Australian troops serving in the armed and peace-keeping forces.

ANITA MORRISH, VICTORIA HILL BRANCH, QLD

½ cup self-raising flour

¾ cup rolled oats (toasted muesli is also good)

½ cup sugar

½ cup desiccated coconut

pinch of salt

1 tablespoon boiling water

55 g butter

1 dessertspoon golden syrup

½ teaspoon bicarbonate of soda

MAKES 20

Preheat the oven to 180°C. Grease baking trays.

Sift flour into a large bowl and mix in oats, sugar, coconut and salt. In a saucepan, combine boiling water with the butter and golden syrup. Bring to the boil and add the bicarb soda. Add liquid to dry ingredients and mix well. Place spoonfuls of mixture on prepared tray and flatten with a floured fork (leave room for spreading). Bake for 10–15 minutes, until golden-brown. Remove from the tray before they harden.

Rock cakes

BERRIS SHARMAN, SPREYTON BRANCH, TAS.

125 g softened butter

125 g dark-brown sugar

1 egg

1 teaspoon honey

1 teaspoon vanilla essence

225 g self-raising flour

2 level tablespoons powdered milk

1 cup mixed dried fruit

MAKES 36

Preheat the oven to 180°C. Grease baking trays.

Cream butter and sugar, then beat in egg, honey and vanilla. Mix in sifted flour and powdered milk, then fruit. Place teaspoonfuls of mixture on prepared trays. Bake for about 15 minutes, until golden-brown.

Malt fancies

JOYCE GOOS, VALENTINE PLAINS BRANCH, QLD

18 malt biscuits, finely crushed

½ × 395-g can condensed milk

55 g chopped almonds

18 pink marshmallows, cut into quarters

55 g dried apricots, chopped

110 g glacé cherries, chopped

55 g raisins, chopped

desiccated coconut, to coat

MAKES 36–40

Combine crushed malt biscuits with condensed milk, almonds, marshmallows, dried apricots, cherries and raisins. Shape the mixture into a sausage shape, then roll in coconut to coat. Chill. Slice once set.

Nut delights

JUDY ANICTOMATIS, DARWIN BRANCH, NT

1 cup plain flour

2 teaspoons cocoa

½ teaspoon bicarbonate of soda

1 cup peanuts

1 cup sugar

1 cup desiccated coconut

125 g butter, melted

1 egg, well beaten

MAKES 24

Preheat the oven to 150°C. Heat a non-stick baking tray.

Sift flour, cocoa and bicarbonate of soda into a bowl. Add all other dry ingredients and mix together, then pour in the melted butter and beaten egg and mix well. Roll mixture into small balls and place on the hot baking tray. Bake for 15–20 minutes.

Ginger Nut bites

ANITA MORRISH, VICTORIA HILL BRANCH, QLD

90 g butter

2 tablespoons golden syrup

½ cup condensed milk

1 teaspoon vanilla essence

1 × 250-g packet Ginger Nut biscuits, crushed

1 cup sultanas

1 cup desiccated coconut, to coat

MAKES ABOUT 50

Melt butter in a large saucepan. Add golden syrup and condensed milk. Over a low heat, stir in vanilla, biscuits and sultanas, and mix until combined.

Roll mixture into balls the size of a walnut, then toss in coconut and refrigerate until firm. Keep covered in the refrigerator.

Crispies

WILMA DELL, DEVONPORT BRANCH, TAS.

125 g softened butter

½ cup sugar

1 egg, beaten

1 cup raisins, sultanas or chopped
   dried apricots

1 cup self-raising flour

corn flakes, to coat

MAKES 24

Preheat the oven to 180°C. Grease a baking tray.

Cream butter and sugar, add egg, then mix in fruit and sifted flour. Make into small balls and roll in corn flakes to coat. Place balls on prepared tray and cook in the oven for 10–15 minutes.

Spice biscuits

MRS. KATHY FRANKCOMBE, SHEFFIELD BRANCH, TAS.

110 g softened butter

¾ cup caster sugar

1 egg, beaten

½ teaspoon vanilla essence

1½ cups self-raising flour

coating

¼ cup caster sugar

1 teaspoon ground cinnamon

½ teaspoon ground nutmeg

MAKES ABOUT 24

Preheat the oven to 180°C. Grease baking trays.

Cream butter and sugar, then beat in egg and vanilla essence. Add sifted flour and mix to form a dough. Roll mixture into balls and toss in the combined sugar, cinnamon and nutmeg, to coat. Place on prepared trays and bake for 10 minutes. Leave on baking tray until cool.

Slices

Fruity wedges

MARY HANSLOW, ORIELTON BRANCH, TAS.

110 g softened butter

1 cup soft brown sugar

1 egg

1½ cups self-raising flour

pinch of salt

½ cup mixed dried fruit

MAKES 24

Preheat oven to 180°C. Grease a 28-cm × 18-cm slice tin.

Cream the butter and sugar, add egg and beat well. Add sifted flour and salt and the mixed fruit. Mix well, then press into prepared tin. Bake for 25–30 minutes. Allow to stand until completely cold before cutting into blocks.

Cream-cheese lattice slice

JOYCE GOOS, VALENTINE PLAINS BRANCH, QLD

125 g softened butter

125 g cream cheese

½ cup sugar

vanilla essence, to taste

1 teaspoon gelatine

2 tablespoons hot water

1½ × 200-g packets lattice biscuits

icing

2 cups icing sugar

lemon juice

MAKES 28

Beat butter and cream cheese, then beat in sugar and vanilla essence. Dissolve the gelatine in the hot water and add to the creamed mixture.

Arrange a layer of lattice biscuits over the base of a slice tin, spread cream-cheese mixture on top, then put another layer of biscuits on top. Refrigerate until set.

Make icing by combining sifted icing sugar with enough lemon juice to make a spreading consistency. Ice the slice with lemon icing.

Jam slice

MRS. ARLENE ROBERTS, MOUNT MORGAN BRANCH, QLD

1 dessertspoon margarine
(a little more if desired)

2 cups self-raising flour

¼ cup sugar (optional)

2 eggs

plum jam, for spreading

½–1 cup desiccated coconut

about 1 dessertspoon sugar

MAKES 15–20

Preheat oven to 180°C. Grease and flour a baking tray.

Rub margarine into sifted flour until it resembles bread crumbs. Add sugar (if using), 1 egg and a little water to make a dough. Spread dough over the tray to cover it. Now spread jam all over the dough, to cover quite well.

In a bowl, combine coconut and remaining egg with sugar to taste, mixing well. Spread the coconut mixture over the jam, covering it completely (the coconut layer should be 5–10 mm thick). Bake until dough is cooked and top is beginning to turn golden-brown. Once cold, cut into squares and store in an airtight container.

Fruit marshmallow squares

This is quite popular for children's birthday parties – a little bit different to chocolate crackles.

JUDY PRATT, DARWIN BRANCH, NT

230 g marshmallows
110 g butter
1 cup seeded raisins
4 cups Rice Bubbles

MAKES 12–18

Melt marshmallows and butter in a large heatproof basin set over a pan of boiling water, stirring frequently until melted. Remove from heat and stir in raisins, then add the Rice Bubbles and mix well. Press the mixture into a greased shallow tin. Refrigerate. Cut into squares when cool and firm.

Ginger slice

HELEN WALL, CANIAMBO BRANCH, VIC.

1 cup sugar

2 tablespoons golden syrup

125 g butter

pinch of salt

1 dessertspoon ground cinnamon

1 dessertspoon ground ginger

1 teaspoon mixed spice

1 egg, well beaten

1 cup sour milk (milk with a
squeeze of lemon juice added)

2 cups plain flour

1 teaspoon bicarbonate of soda

1 cup chopped raisins

MAKES 18–24

Preheat the oven to 180°C. Grease a slice tin.

Combine sugar, syrup, butter, salt and spices in a large saucepan and heat until melted and combined. Add egg and sour milk and mix. Sift together flour and soda, then stir into spice mixture. Add raisins and mix well. Put into prepared tin and bake for about 30 minutes.

White Christmas

JOYCE GOOS, VALENTINE PLAINS BRANCH, QLD

½ cup copha, melted

2 cups Rice Bubbles

½ cup icing sugar

1 cup powdered milk

1 cup desiccated coconut

1 cup mixed crystallised cherries, crystallised ginger, and white and milk chocolate chips

MAKES 36

Combine melted copha with Rice Bubbles, sifted icing sugar and powdered milk, coconut, and cherries, ginger and chocolate. Press mixture into a slice tray. Refrigerate until set, then cut into squares.

Apple slice

This slice has been very popular at soup and sandwich luncheons and at market stalls.

MARION SPAULDING, HIGHCROFT/STORMLEA BRANCH, TAS.

1 × 340-g packet homebrand butter cake mix

100 g butter or margarine, melted

1 × 425-g can pie apples, drained (or 1½ cups drained stewed apples)

1 × 300–400-ml tub sour cream

2 eggs, lightly beaten

2 tablespoons grated lemon zest (optional)

1 tablespoon ground cinnamon

MAKES 32

Preheat the oven to 180°C. Line the base and sides of a 30-cm × 20-cm slice tin with baking paper, making sure the paper extends up the sides of the tin.

Do not follow the instructions on the cake mix packet – instead, combine cake mix with the melted butter or margarine and mix well. Press mixture into prepared tin. Cook for about 15 minutes or until lightly browned. Remove but leave oven on. Cool base slightly, then spread apple over to cover.

Beat sour cream, eggs and lemon zest (if using) until smooth, then pour mixture over the apples. Bake for about 30 minutes or until custard is set. Sprinkle the top with cinnamon. Allow to cool in the tin, then refrigerate until cold. Cut into squares to serve.

Variations
Add ½ cup sultanas or 1 cup desiccated coconut to the cake mix, along with 25 g extra melted butter.

Cherry and walnut slice

MARY HANSLOW, ORIELTON BRANCH, TAS.

110 g softened butter or margarine

110 g soft brown sugar (I use a little less)

1 large dessertspoon golden syrup

1 egg

55 g self-raising flour

170 g plain flour

1 cup sultanas or dried fruit of your choice

a few glacé cherries and walnuts, chopped, for the top

MAKES 24

Preheat oven to 180°C. Grease a 20-cm × 25-cm slice tin.

Cream butter and sugar well, then add golden syrup, egg, sifted flours and fruit. Mix well. Press mixture into prepared tin and sprinkle with chopped cherries and walnuts. Bake in the oven for 15–20 minutes. Cut into squares when cold.

Chocolate slice 1

This is a rich-tasting slice.

VALERIE TITLEY, PEGARAH KING ISLAND BRANCH, TAS.

base

185 g butter, melted

1 cup self-raising flour

1 cup desiccated coconut

½ cup soft brown sugar

topping

110 g marshmallows

125 g chocolate, chopped

⅓ cup milk

2 teaspoons gelatine

2 tablespoons rum or water

300 ml cream

MAKES 12–16

Preheat the oven to 180°C. Grease a lamington tin.

For the base, simply mix all ingredients together. Place mixture in the prepared tin and bake for 25 minutes.

To make the topping, place marshmallows, chocolate and milk in a saucepan and cook over gentle heat until melted. Combine gelatine with the rum or water, then stir into the chocolate mix. Allow to cool. Whip the cream, then fold into the chocolate mixture. Pour topping over the cooled base and refrigerate until set.

Chocolate slice 2

DULCIE FRENCH, CENTRAL COAST BRANCH, TAS.

a good 150 g softened butter

½ cup sugar

1 cup self-raising flour

1 tablespoon cocoa

1 cup corn flakes

1 cup desiccated coconut

MAKES 16

Preheat the oven to 180°C. Grease a slice tin.

Cream butter and sugar, then add sifted flour and cocoa, corn flakes and coconut. Put into prepared tin and cook for 30 minutes. Ice when cool if desired (you could use chocolate, plain, mint or another icing of your choice).

Peppermint chocolate slice

WILMA DELL, DEVONPORT BRANCH, TAS.

125 g butter

1 tablespoon cocoa

250 g chocolate chips

2 tablespoons golden syrup

250 g sweet biscuits, crushed

topping

375 g white cooking chocolate, chopped

10–12 drops peppermint flavouring

dark or milk chocolate (optional)

MAKES 18–24

Combine all slice ingredients (with the exception of the biscuits) in a saucepan and melt. Add biscuits and mix to combine. Press firmly into a 30-cm × 19-cm tray.

To make the topping, melt the white chocolate in a heat-proof bowl set over a pan of simmering water (or in the microwave), then stir in peppermint flavouring. Spread topping over slice when cold. A small amount of brown chocolate can be melted and drizzled over the top to decorate if desired.

Chocolate gingers

JOYCE GOOS, VALENTINE PLAINS BRANCH, QLD

2½ cups icing sugar

4 tablespoons cocoa

4 tablespoons powdered milk

100 g crystallised ginger, finely chopped

230 g copha, melted

MAKES 30

Sift together icing sugar, cocoa and powdered milk, then add ginger and melted copha. Spread into a greased slice tin. Refrigerate. Cut into squares once set.

Quick and easy slice

P. SAUNDERS, SELBOURNE BRANCH, TAS.

230 g butter

3 tablespoons jam (any flavour)

3 cups self-raising flour

1 cup sugar

plain icing (page 180)

MAKES 14–28

Preheat the oven to 180°C. Grease a lamington tin.

Melt butter and jam together in a small saucepan. Sift flour and sugar into a bowl and mix in the butter and jam. Place mixture in prepared tin and bake for 25 minutes. Ice with plain icing when cool.

Chester cake

The pastry in this recipe is very good for making apple slice as well.

HELEN WALL, CANIAMBO BRANCH, VIC.

pastry

125 g softened butter

125 g caster sugar

1 egg

125 g plain flour

125 g self-raising flour

filling

½ cup sultanas

1½ cups dates, chopped

2 teaspoons ground cinnamon

3 teaspoons golden syrup

2 teaspoons boiling water

MAKES 24

Preheat oven to 180°C. Grease a 23-cm × 28-cm slice tin.

Cream butter and sugar, then beat in egg. Sift flours together then add to creamed mixture and work to a soft dough. Roll out half the pastry and use to line the base of the prepared tin.

To make the filling, combine all ingredients. Spread filling evenly over the pastry.

Roll out remaining pastry and use to cover the filling. Prick the surface with a fork.

Cook for about 20 minutes, until golden-brown.

Fruit squares

BERRIS SHARMAN, SPREYTON BRANCH, TAS.

230 g copha

1 tablespoon rum essence

2½ cups Rice Bubbles

1 cup powdered milk

1 cup icing sugar

1 cup sultanas

½ cup chopped sweet preserved
   ginger

½ cup chopped glacé cherries

1 tablespoon cocoa

MAKES 24

Melt copha, add rum essence, then mix with all other ingredients. Press mixture into a 18-cm × 28-cm slab tin. Refrigerate. When set, cut into squares.

Apricot and date slice

MARY HANSLOW, ORIELTON BRANCH, TAS.

¾ cup chopped dried apricots

230 g self-raising flour

pinch of salt

1 cup soft brown sugar

¾ cup desiccated coconut,
  plus extra for sprinkling

½ cup chopped dates

170 g butter, melted

lemon icing (page 179)

MAKES 48

Preheat the oven to 180°C. Grease a 25-cm × 36-cm scone tray.

Cover apricots with boiling water and leave to soak for about 20 minutes, then drain. Sift flour and salt into a mixing bowl, add sugar, coconut and chopped apricots and dates. Pour in melted butter and mix well.

Press into prepared tin and bake for 25 minutes. Allow to cool in the tin, then ice with lemon icing and sprinkle with coconut. Cut into finger-length pieces.

Granny's choc-chip slice

This recipe is one I have been baking for 35 years. (Cook's tip: If you have a resourceful child or two, the choc-chip packet may be safely hidden inside the powdered milk box under the bag of milk. Ours didn't go AWOL in 16 years.)

CHRISTINE TYSON, LUCASTON BRANCH, TAS.

125 g softened butter

125 g raw sugar

60 g white sugar

1 teaspoon vanilla essence

1 egg

125 g self-raising flour

125 g wholemeal self-raising flour

60 g walnuts

60 g chocolate chips

MAKES 24

Preheat the oven to 180°C (or 170°C fan-forced). Line a lamington or slice tin (approximately 24-cm × 31-cm) with baking paper.

Cream the butter with the sugars and vanilla essence (I use a free-standing mixer). Beat in egg, then add sifted flours, walnuts and choc chips and mix well. Place mixture into prepared tin and smooth with a wet hand. Bake for 30 minutes. Cut into fingers while still in the tin, then leave until cool enough to handle. Tip out onto a cake rack.

Variation
Instead of the walnuts, you can use 60 g almonds and 60 g chopped dates.

Fruit slice 1

This slice is very quick to make and great for unexpected visitors. It is one of many recipes passed down to me from my mother before I left home.

JUDY PRATT, DARWIN BRANCH, NT

110 g margarine, melted

¾ cup soft brown sugar

1 egg

1 cup self-raising flour

1 cup mixed dried fruit

125 g walnuts (half a 250-g packet)

orange or vanilla icing (pages 179 and 180)

desiccated coconut, for sprinkling (optional)

MAKES 18–20

Preheat the oven to 180°C. Grease a Swiss roll tin.

Combine melted margarine with the sugar, then allow to cool. Break in the egg and mix with a wooden spoon. Add sifted flour, mixed fruit and walnuts. Place in prepared tin and bake for 25 minutes.

While slice is still warm, ice with orange or vanilla icing and cut into fingers. (Coconut sprinkled on top is nice for a change.)

Fruit slice 2

JOYCE GOOS, VALENTINE PLAINS BRANCH, QLD

110 g butter

2 teaspoons golden syrup

1 cup dates or raisins

1 cup desiccated coconut

1 cup self-raising flour

½ cup sugar

icing

2 cups icing sugar

lemon juice

MAKES 24

Preheat the oven to 180°C. Grease a slice tin.

Melt butter and golden syrup in a small saucepan. In a mixing bowl, combine dates or raisins, coconut, sifted flour and sugar. Pour in butter mixture and combine. Press mixture into the prepared slice tin and bake for 20 minutes.

Make icing by combining sifted icing sugar with enough lemon juice to make a spreading consistency.

While the slice is still warm, spread with the lemon icing.

Fudge

JANET AVERY, LATROBE BRANCH, TAS.

1¾ cups self-raising flour

4 heaped teaspoons cocoa

pinch of salt

½ cup milk

¼ teaspoon vanilla essence

110 g softened butter

1½ cups sugar

2 eggs

¾ cup boiling water

chocolate icing (page 179)

MAKES 12–16

Preheat the oven to 180°C. Grease a 19-cm × 19-cm tin.

Sift together the flour, cocoa and salt. In a separate bowl combine the milk and vanilla. Cream the butter and sugar in a large bowl, beat in eggs, then gradually beat in the milk mixture and dry ingredients. Once combined, mix in the boiling water. Put mixture into prepared tin and bake for 35 minutes.

Allow fudge to cool, then invert onto a plate. Ice with chocolate icing.

(Note: instead of a traditional chocolate icing, I often use an icing made by combining low-fat cream cheese or ricotta with a dash of vanilla essence and enough cocoa to give a rich brown colour.)

Weet-Bix fudge

EILEEN McMULLEN, RANELAGH BRANCH, TAS.

125 g butter

2 tablespoons milk

1 cup sugar

7 Weet-Bix biscuits, crushed

5 tablespoons powdered milk

2 tablespoons cocoa

1 cup desiccated coconut, plus
   extra for sprinkling

MAKES 24

Boil butter, milk and sugar in a saucepan. Combine Weet-Bix with other dry ingredients in a bowl and pour milk mixture over. Mix well. Press into a 18-cm × 28-cm tin. Sprinkle coconut on top and chill in the fridge. When set, cut into squares.

Over-the-top fudge brownies

These are a big crowd pleaser and deliver a huge chocolate punch. I passed this recipe on to a friend, who sent some, vacuum-packed, to her partner serving with the armed forces in Afghanistan – he said they were the best-tasting treat any of them had ever received in the mail.

MELISSA ANICTOMATIS, PORT DARWIN BRANCH, NT

200 g dark cooking chocolate

200 g butter

4 eggs

1 cup caster sugar

1 teaspoon vanilla essence

1⅓ cups plain flour

¼ cup cocoa

¾ cup dark chocolate chips

¾ cup milk chocolate chips

⅓ cup white chocolate chips

drinking chocolate powder, to dust

MAKES 20

Preheat the oven to 180°C. Brush a shallow 20-cm × 30-cm tin with oil and line with baking paper (allowing it to extend up over the two long sides).

Melt the cooking chocolate and butter in a heatproof bowl set over a saucepan of simmering water (or in the microwave). Leave to cool slightly.

Beat the eggs, sugar and vanilla essence with an electric mixer, or by hand with a wire whisk. Add to the chocolate mixture along with the sifted flour and cocoa. Stir with a wooden spoon until just combined. Combine dark and milk choc chips in a bowl, then add half to the brownie mixture and stir to combine. Add all the white choc chips to the mixture and stir to combine.

Pour batter into the prepared tin. Sprinkle the remaining choc chips over the top and press in lightly with the palm of your hand. Bake for 45–50 minutes. Cool completely in the tin, then refrigerate for 2–3 hours, until firm. Cut into squares and dust with drinking chocolate.

Chocolate date slice

This is a good recipe to make for the shearers because it goes a long way and is easy to make as it is all done in the one saucepan.

HELEN WALL, CANIAMBO BRANCH, VIC.

1 cup chopped dates

125 g butter

1 cup sugar

1 egg, beaten

1¾ cups plain flour

½ teaspoon bicarbonate
of soda

1 teaspoon baking powder

1 teaspoon ground cinnamon

1½ tablespoons cocoa

pinch of salt

½ cup chopped walnuts

chocolate icing (page 179)

MAKES 30

Preheat oven to 180°C. Grease a 25-cm × 30-cm tin.

Place dates and 1 cup water in a large saucepan and bring to the boil. Remove from the heat, stir in butter until melted, then allow to cool until lukewarm. Stir in sugar and egg.

Sift together the flour, bicarb soda, baking powder, cinnamon, cocoa and salt, then add to the date mixture and mix. Stir in nuts. Pour mixture into prepared tin and bake for 20 minutes. Cool, then ice with chocolate icing.

Lorna's ginger delight

ELAINE YOUD, DEVONPORT BRANCH, TAS.

230 g coffee biscuits, crushed

1 × 395-g can condensed milk

1 cup sweet preserved ginger

1 teaspoon ground ginger

½ cup desiccated coconut

3 tablespoons cocoa

icing

110 g copha, melted

70 g icing sugar

1½ tablespoons cocoa

MAKES 24

Line a slab tin with foil or grease well.

Mix all slice ingredients together. Press into the slab tin.

To make the icing, combine melted copha with the sifted icing sugar and cocoa. Mix well, then spread over the slice. Refrigerate until set.

Chocolate rough slice

MARY HANSLOW, ORIELTON BRANCH, TAS.

base

1 cup self-raising flour

1 dessertspoon cocoa

pinch of salt

⅓ cup caster sugar

¼ cup desiccated coconut

110 g butter, melted

chocolate rough topping

½ × 395-g can condensed milk

1 tablespoon cocoa

1 cup icing sugar

1½ tablespoons butter, melted

1 cup desiccated coconut

1 teaspoon vanilla essence

MAKES 24

Preheat the oven to 180°C. Line an 18-cm × 28-cm lamington tin with baking paper.

To make the base, sift flour, cocoa and salt into a basin. Stir in sugar and coconut, then add melted butter and mix well. Press into prepared lamington tin and bake for 25 minutes.

For the topping, simply combine all ingredients in a basin and mix well.

Cool the cake base slightly. Cover with the chocolate rough mixture while it's still warm and set aside. Cut into slices when cold.

Pecan slice

JOYCE GOOS, VALENTINE PLAINS BRANCH, QLD

½ cup butter, melted
½ cup soft brown sugar
½ cup desiccated coconut
½ cup finely chopped pecan nuts
1 cup self-raising flour
lemon icing (page 179)

MAKES 24

Preheat the oven to 180°C. Grease a slice tin.

Allow melted butter to cool, then combine in a bowl with the sugar, coconut and chopped pecans. Sift in the self-raising flour and mix well. Press mixture into prepared slice tin and bake for 20 minutes. Ice with lemon icing while still warm.

Coconut fingers

MARY HANSLOW, ORIELTON BRANCH, TAS.

topping

110 g desiccated coconut

½ cup sugar

1 egg

pinch of salt

base

110 g self-raising flour

85 g plain flour

pinch of salt

85 g butter, cut into pieces

85 g sugar

1 egg, beaten

fruit jam (raspberry, apricot, etc.),
    for spreading

MAKES 24–30

Preheat the oven to 180°C. If you want the slice to have a thick base, grease a 28-cm × 18-cm slice tin. If you prefer a thin base, grease a 35-cm × 38-cm baking tray.

To make the topping, mix all ingredients together.

For the base, sift flours and salt together, then rub in butter, add sugar and mix in the beaten egg to achieve a stiff dough. Knead well, then roll out thinly.

Place dough into prepared baking tin, cover with a layer of jam, then spread on the topping mixture. Bake for about 20 minutes. Remove from oven, but leave on the baking tray until fairly cool. Cut into fingers to serve.

Apricot slice 1

JOYCE GOOS, VALENTINE PLAINS BRANCH, QLD

base

2 tablespoons softened butter

½ cup sugar

1 egg

1½ cups self-raising flour

apricot jam, for spreading

topping

1 egg, beaten

1 cup sugar

1 cup desiccated coconut

MAKES 24

Preheat the oven to 180°C. Grease a slice tin.

Cream butter and sugar. Beat in egg. Sift in the flour and mix well. Press mixture into prepared slice tin. Spread with apricot jam.

To make the topping, combine the egg, sugar and coconut in a bowl. Mix well, then spread over the base. Bake for 30 minutes.

Apricot slice 2

WILMA DELL, DEVONPORT BRANCH, TAS.

125 g butter

80 g soft brown sugar

½ × 395-g can condensed milk

1 × 200-g packet sweet biscuits, crushed

1 cup dried apricots, chopped

desiccated coconut, for sprinkling

MAKES 18–24

Heat butter and sugar in a saucepan until melted, then add condensed milk, biscuits and apricots. Press mixture into a 30-cm × 19-cm tin. Sprinkle with coconut and cool in the fridge until set.

Apricot slice 3

DULCIE FRENCH, CENTRAL COAST BRANCH, TAS.

110 g softened butter

1 cup sugar

2 eggs

1 cup plain flour

¾ cup desiccated coconut

1 cup finely chopped dried apricots

½ cup milk

lemon icing (page 179) (optional)

MAKES 24

Preheat the oven to 180°C. Grease an 18-cm × 28-cm slice tin.

Cream butter and sugar, then beat in eggs. Mix in sifted flour, coconut and apricots. Add milk and mix well. Place mixture in prepared tin and bake for 30 minutes. Once cooled, ice with lemon icing if desired. Cut into slices to serve.

Easy apricot slice

This is a great pantry recipe as it is just a simple cake mix with tinned apricots added.

MELISSA ANICTOMATIS, PORT DARWIN BRANCH, NT

1½ cups plain flour

¾ cup caster sugar, plus extra
for sprinkling

1 teaspoon baking powder

pinch of salt

3 eggs

¼ cup milk

2 teaspoons vanilla extract

180 g softened butter

14 apricots, peeled, stoned and
halved (or you can use tinned)

MAKES 14

Preheat oven to 160°C. Grease and line a 20-cm × 30-cm lamington tin (or use a non-stick tin).

Sift the flour, sugar, baking powder and salt into a large bowl and make a well in the centre. Place eggs, milk and vanilla in another bowl and mix to combine. Pour the egg mixture into the well in the dry ingredients, add the butter and beat with electric beaters for 2 minutes, until smooth. Spread mixture evenly into prepared tin. Push apricot halves cut-side up into the mixture, arranging them in neat rows.

Place in the oven and bake for 20 minutes. Sprinkle with about 2 tablespoons extra sugar, then return to the oven and cook for another 20 minutes, or until a skewer inserted into the centre comes out clean. Cut into fingers, with two apricot halves per slice.

Ginger and walnut slice

This is one of my favourite recipes to make for my grandchildren at Christmas time.

HEATHER J. COOPER, DEVONPORT BRANCH, TAS.

2 × 250-g packets malt biscuits, crushed

1 × 395-g can condensed milk

1 cup walnuts (2 cups if you like walnuts)

1 × 375-g packet low-fat glacé ginger

230 g butter, melted

¾ cup soft brown sugar

2 teaspoons ground ginger

2 teaspoons vanilla essence

melted chocolate, for topping

MAKES ABOUT 60

Put all ingredients (except chocolate) in a bowl and mix well. Press into a slice tin and top with melted chocolate. Allow to cool a little, then put into the bottom of the fridge to set. Cut into small squares to serve.

Mothers' Day slice

MARY HANSLOW, ORIELTON BRANCH, TAS.

110 g butter or margarine

1 cup sugar

1 egg

1 cup self-raising flour

1 tablespoon cocoa

pinch of salt

½ cup desiccated coconut

2 tablespoons milk

½ teaspoon vanilla essence

raspberry jam, for spreading

chocolate sprinkles and desiccated coconut (toasted if desired), for sprinkling

marshmallow

1 tablespoon gelatine

1 cup sugar

1 tablespoon lemon juice

few drops vanilla essence

MAKES 24

Preheat the oven to 180°C. Grease an 18-cm × 28-cm lamington tin.

Melt butter in a saucepan, then remove from heat, add sugar and mix until sugar is dissolved. Add egg and mix well. Stir in sifted flour, cocoa and salt, coconut, milk and vanilla. Spread mixture into prepared lamington tin. Bake for 15–20 minutes. Remove from the oven and spread the cooked base with raspberry jam. Set aside to cool.

To make the marshmallow topping, soak the gelatine in ¼ cup water. Put the sugar and another ¼ cup water in a saucepan and heat gently, stirring constantly. Add the gelatine and boil for 5 minutes, allow to cool a little, then add lemon juice and vanilla. Beat until thick and white and just starting to set. Pour over the cooked base and sprinkle with chocolate sprinkles and coconut. Cut into fingers to serve.

Banana slice

JUDY ANICTOMATIS, DARWIN BRANCH, NT

1 cup self-raising flour

½ teaspoon ground cinnamon

½ teaspoon ground nutmeg or cloves

60 g softened butter or margarine

½ cup sugar

1 banana, mashed

1 egg

¼ cup milk

¼ cup chopped walnuts

icing

1 tablespoon butter, melted

1 teaspoon hot water

lemon juice, to taste

icing sugar

MAKES 12

Preheat oven to 180°C. Grease a 15-cm × 25-cm slice tin.

Sift flour and spices into a bowl. In a separate bowl, cream butter and sugar, then add the mashed banana and beat for 2 minutes. Add the egg and beat well. Mix in the milk and flour mixture alternately. Stir in the walnuts. Put into prepared tin and bake for 25–30 minutes.

To make the icing, combine the butter with the water and lemon juice and add sufficient sifted icing sugar to achieve the desired consistency.

While slice is still warm, spread with lemon icing and cut into squares.

Chocolate cherry delights

PHYLLIS HINGSTON, SASSAFRAS/WESLEY VALE BRANCH, TAS.

125 g butter

½ cup sugar

2 tablespoons cocoa

¼ cup desiccated coconut

1 egg, beaten

1½ cups chopped glacé cherries

2 cups crushed sweet biscuits

2 teaspoons vanilla essence

icing

1 cup icing sugar

1 tablespoon plus 1 teaspoon
  cocoa

1 tablespoon boiling water

1 teaspoon vanilla essence

MAKES 24

Melt butter in a medium-sized saucepan. Add sugar and cocoa and blend in. Remove from heat and stir in coconut, egg, cherries, biscuit crumbs and vanilla essence. Put mixture into a Swiss roll tin and refrigerate.

To make icing, sift together icing sugar and cocoa, then mix in boiling water and vanilla.

Ice the slice when cooled, then cut into squares.

Afternoon tea fingers

This is my mum's recipe.

MRS. ANNETTE FERGUSSON, ORIELTON BRANCH, TAS.

pastry base

60 g butter or margarine,
  cut into pieces

125 g self-raising flour

1–2 tablespoons milk

raspberry or apricot jam,
  for spreading

sponge

60 g softened butter

1 cup sugar

2 eggs

1¼ cups self-raising flour

¼ cup milk

½ teaspoon vanilla essence

icing

1 cup icing sugar

3 teaspoons butter

¼ teaspoon vanilla essence

about 1 tablespoon hot water

MAKES 24

Preheat the oven to 190°C. Grease a Swiss roll tin.

To make the pastry, rub butter into sifted flour until crumbs form. Add just enough milk to make a workable dough. Roll out the dough and use it to line the prepared tin. Spread with jam.

To make the sponge, cream the butter and sugar, then add eggs one at a time, beating well after each addition. Add sifted flour, milk and vanilla and beat to form a creamy batter. Pour mixture over the pastry base. Bake the slice for 30 minutes. Remove from the oven and set aside to cool.

Make the butter icing by combining sifted icing sugar with butter, vanilla and enough hot water to make a spreading consistency.

Ice when slice is cold. Cut into fingers to serve.

(Note: passionfruit butter icing is also very nice with this slice – just use a couple of tablespoons of passionfruit pulp in the icing instead of the vanilla and hot water.)

Trifle slice

This slice is also nice made with seasonal berries instead of peaches.

BARBARA GIBBONS, CENTRAL COAST BRANCH, TAS.

1 jam roll, cut into thin slices

sweet sherry

1 × 825-g can peaches, drained and diced

2 × packets Aeroplane Jelly Lite Port Wine jelly crystals (each packet has 2 × 9-g sachets)

desiccated coconut, for sprinkling

blancmange

600 ml milk

2 tablespoons sugar

5 level tablespoons cornflour

pinch of salt

1 teaspoon butter

3 or 4 drops lemon essence

MAKES 12

Arrange the jam roll slices over a 23-cm × 32-cm tray and sprinkle with sweet sherry. Spread peaches on top of the layered jam roll slices. Place jelly crystals from four sachets in a bowl and mix with 4 cups boiling water and 2 cups cold water. Let jelly cool, then carefully pour it over the peaches. Put in the fridge to set.

To make the blancmange, combine 50 ml of the milk with the sugar, cornflour and salt. Combine this mixture with remaining milk in a small saucepan and add butter. Stir over gentle heat until thick and creamy. Remove from heat and add lemon essence. Set aside to cool, then spread mixture over the set jelly. Sprinkle coconut on top and put back in the fridge to set.

When firmly set, cut into slices and decorate if you wish.

Arrowroot slice

A little bit of this slice goes a long way!

HEATHER J. COOPER, DEVONPORT BRANCH, TAS.

110 g butter

1 cup sugar

1 egg

1 tablespoon cocoa

pinch of salt

1 tablespoon vanilla essence

1½ cups sultanas

1 cup walnuts or slivered almonds

1 cup glacé cherries

1 × 250-g packet arrowroot biscuits (or biscuits to your liking), crushed

MAKES 40

Melt butter in a saucepan, then add all other ingredients (except crushed biscuits) and mix well. Bring just to the boil, then add the crushed biscuits and stir to combine. Press mixture into a slice tin. Leave to cool, then chill in the fridge for about an hour. Cut into squares.

Kate's slice

This is my husband's favourite slice. I have experimented with the recipe over the years – the crushed pineapple makes it.

SHIRLEY PLATZ, MIDDLE RIDGE BRANCH, QLD

base

1 cup self-raising flour

½ cup sugar

½ cup desiccated coconut

125 g butter, melted

topping

¼ cup self-raising flour

½ cup sugar

½ cup desiccated coconut

½ cup sultanas

½ cup crushed pineapple, drained

2 eggs, lightly beaten

MAKES 24

Preheat oven to 180°C. Grease and line an 18-cm × 28-cm slice tin.

In a large bowl, combine sifted flour, sugar and coconut. Stir in butter. Press mixture firmly into prepared tin. Bake for 10 minutes (at this point it will be half-cooked). Remove and leave oven on.

To make the topping, sift flour and sugar into a large bowl. Add remaining ingredients and mix well. Pour topping over the base. Bake for another 25–30 minutes, until golden-brown and firm to touch. Cut into squares and serve warm or cold.

Strawberry slice

P. SAUNDERS, SELBOURNE BRANCH, TAS.

250 g softened unsalted butter

250 g cream cheese

1 cup caster sugar

3 teaspoons vanilla essence

2 level teaspoons gelatine, dissolved in a little boiling water

1 × 250-g punnet strawberries, sliced

1 × 200-g packet lattice biscuits

MAKES 12

Cream butter, cream cheese and sugar, then add vanilla and dissolved gelatine and beat well. Add a few sliced strawberries.

Line the base of a 54-cm × 40-cm tin or plastic dish with lattice biscuits, then pour half the creamed mixture over the biscuits. Arrange remaining strawberry slices over the cheese mix, then pour remaining mixture on top. Place in the fridge to set. Cut into slices to serve.

Louise slice

This recipe has been in my family for three or four generations and it is still a favourite.

JULIE CHAPPEL, MILLOO BRANCH, VIC.

110 g softened butter

¼ cup sugar

2 egg yolks (plus 1 extra egg
  if needed)

285 g plain flour

1 teaspoon baking powder

jam, for spreading (I use the family
  favourite of homemade plum
  and raspberry)

topping

2 egg whites

½ cup caster sugar

110 g desiccated coconut

MAKES 24

Preheat the oven to 180°C. Line a Swiss roll tin with baking paper.

Cream butter and sugar, then beat in egg yolks and extra egg (if using). Sift together flour and baking powder and add to the creamed mixture, mixing well. Press into prepared Swiss roll tin and spread with jam.

To make the topping, beat egg whites until stiff, then add caster sugar and coconut and mix. Spread topping over the base. Bake for 20–25 minutes.

Beatie slice

This was my grandfather's favourite slice recipe.

HELEN WALL, CANIAMBO BRANCH, VIC.

3 cups rolled oats
½ cup sugar
¼ cup slivered almonds
150 g butter, melted

MAKES 24

Preheat the oven to 180°C. Grease a slice tin.

Mix oats, sugar and almonds in a bowl. Pour the melted butter over and mix well.

Place mixture into the prepared slice tin and bake for about 15 minutes.

Orange spice bars

PATRICIA WALKER, GEORGE TOWN BRANCH, TAS.

½ cup softened butter
or margarine

¾ cup raw sugar

2 eggs

grated zest of 1 orange

1 tablespoon orange juice

1½ cups plain flour

1½ teaspoons baking powder

1 teaspoon mixed spice

½ teaspoon ground cloves

¾ cup sultanas

¾ cup chopped walnuts

lemon or orange icing (page 179)

MAKES 20

Preheat the oven to 180°C. Grease a 23-cm × 30-cm or 23-cm × 25-cm slice tin.

Cream butter or margarine until smooth, then gradually beat in sugar until light and fluffy. Beat in eggs with orange zest and juice. Sift dry ingredients together, then blend into the creamed mixture. Fold in sultanas and walnuts. Spread into prepared tin and bake for approximately 30 minutes. Cool slightly after removing from oven, then cut into fingers. Ice with orange or lemon icing when bars are cold.

Rhubarb slice

Also known as 'what to do when you have too much rhubarb in the garden'! Even people who don't like rhubarb usually really enjoy this slice. (Don't be tempted to use cooked rhubarb – raw rhubarb may be hard to stir, but it gets soft when cooked. And don't use any extra ingredients.)

JANE BEAVAN, ROCHES BEACH BRANCH, TAS.

60 g softened butter

2 cups soft brown sugar

2 eggs

1 teaspoon vanilla essence

2 cups plain flour

1 teaspoon bicarbonate of soda

1 teaspoon salt

250 g sour cream

500 g chopped raw rhubarb

MAKES 16–20

Preheat the oven to 180°C. Grease two 23-cm x 25-cm slice tins.

Beat together butter, sugar, eggs and vanilla. Stir in the sifted dry ingredients, then add sour cream and finally stir in the rhubarb. Put into prepared tins and bake for 1 hour. Cut into squares to serve.

Ginger crisp

If you want a thicker topping you can double the mixture.

MARY HANSLOW, ORIELTON BRANCH, TAS.

110 g softened butter

¼ cup sugar

1 cup self-raising flour

1 level teaspoon ground ginger

topping

1 dessertspoon butter

1 dessertspoon golden syrup

2 tablespoons icing sugar

MAKES 24

Preheat oven to 190°C. Grease a 20-cm × 25-cm slice tin.

Cream butter and sugar, then add sifted flour and ginger and mix well. Press mixture into prepared tin. Place slice into preheated oven and *turn oven off*. Leave biscuits to cook in the oven for 15–20 minutes.

To make the topping, combine all ingredients in a small saucepan and heat gently, stirring all the time. When hot, pour over the cooked slice. Allow to set.

Robyn Shea's no-bake slice

This recipe was given to me by Robyn Shea (Kumbia Branch, Queensland).

MARIAN MUDRA, KUMBIA BRANCH, QLD

230 g desiccated coconut, plus extra for sprinkling

110 g butter, melted

1 × 250-g packet Marie biscuits, crushed

½ × 395-g can condensed milk

juice and zest of 1 lemon

lemon or plain icing (pages 179 and 180)

MAKES 20

Mix all ingredients together and press into a slice tin. Ice with plain or lemon icing and sprinkle with extra coconut. Cut into slices to serve.

Nougat slice

AILSA BOND A.M., RIVERSIDE BRANCH, TAS.

85 g softened butter

¾ cup sugar

1 egg, well beaten

1 cup self-raising flour

¾ cup mixed dates and chopped nuts

icing

90 g softened butter

1 cup soft icing mixture

3 teaspoons milk

vanilla essence, to taste (optional)

MAKES 16

Preheat the oven to 180°C. Grease a slice tin.

To make the slice, cream butter and sugar, then beat in egg. Stir in sifted flour, dates and nuts. Spread mixture in prepared tin and bake for 30 minutes. Transfer to cooling rack.

To make the icing, cream the butter until light and fluffy. Add the sifted icing mixture, milk, and a little vanilla essence if desired. Beat until soft and smooth.

Ice when slice is cold.

(Note: soft icing mixture can be purchased at most supermarkets.)

Caramel squares

BERRIS SHARMAN, SPREYTON BRANCH, TAS.

110 g margarine or butter

110 g soft brown sugar

1 egg, beaten

1 teaspoon vanilla essence

1 cup dates

½ cup walnuts

1 cup self-raising flour

MAKES 24

Preheat the oven to 180°C. Grease a slab tin.

Melt margarine or butter, then cream with the sugar. Beat in egg and vanilla. Add all other ingredients and mix well. Put into prepared tin and bake for 20–30 minutes. Cut into squares when cool.

Snowball surprise cakes

I make these each Christmas for gifts – three or four on a small plate. They keep well in an airtight container in the fridge.

ALWYN HILLS, WYNYARD BRANCH, TAS.

30 g gelatine

2 cups sugar, plus a little extra

2 egg whites

approximately 1 tablespoon cocoa

¾–1 cup warm milk

desiccated coconut, to coat

MAKES 36

Add gelatine to a saucepan with 2 cups cold water and the sugar and boil for 20 minutes. Set aside to cool. Beat the egg whites until stiff. When gelatine mixture is cool, add the egg whites and beat until mixture is very stiff. Pour into a square or oblong dish and leave to set. Cut into squares when firm.

Combine the cocoa, milk and a little sugar. Dip squares into the chocolate mixture to coat, then roll in coconut. Leave to dry on a cake rack until the coating hardens.

(Note: the snowball cakes are better served a day after making.)

Elgin Vale slice

I first tasted this slice when visiting the QCWA branch at Elgin Vale some eight years ago.

MARIAN MUDRA, KUMBIA BRANCH, QLD

1 × 470-g packet vanilla cake mix

1 × 450-g or 500-g can pie apples (or use apricots, sliced peaches or fruit salad), drained

300 ml yoghurt or sour cream

1 egg, beaten

ground cinnamon, for sprinkling (optional)

MAKES ABOUT 12

Preheat the oven to 180°C. Grease a slice tin.

Make up vanilla cake mixture, following directions on the packet (this may require egg and/or milk or water, depending on the brand you are using). Spread batter over the base of the prepared tin, then cover evenly with the tinned fruit. Mix the yoghurt or sour cream with the beaten egg and spread this over the fruit. Bake for 25–30 minutes. Sprinkle with cinnamon if desired, then cut into squares.

Tan squares

JOYCE GOOS, VALENTINE PLAINS BRANCH, QLD

base

170 g butter, melted

285 g plain flour

1 teaspoon baking powder

85 g sugar

topping

55 g butter

½ × 395-g can condensed milk

2 tablespoons golden syrup

MAKES 24

Preheat the oven to 175°C. Grease a slice tin.

For the base, combine melted butter with the sifted flour and baking powder, and the sugar. Mix well. Chill a quarter of the mixture and press remainder into prepared slice tin.

To make the topping, heat the butter in a small saucepan with the condensed milk and golden syrup. Pour over the prepared base. Grate the chilled reserved base mixture over the top. Bake for about 35 minutes. Cut into squares when cold.

Apricot shortbread slice

JANET AVERY, LATROBE BRANCH, TAS.

shortbread

110 g butter

230 g self-raising flour

2 tablespoons sweetener
or sugar

2 egg yolks

topping

170 g dried apricots

sweetener or sugar, to taste

2 egg whites

MAKES 16

Preheat oven to 180°C. Grease a 19-cm × 19-cm slice tin.

Rub butter into flour, then mix in sweetener or sugar and egg yolks. Add a little water, a tiny bit at a time, until you have a dough consistency. Press into prepared tin and bake for 15 minutes. Remove from the oven and allow to cool. (Leave oven on.)

While shortbread is cooking, start making the topping by stewing the apricots in a little water, with sweetener or sugar to taste, until tender. Drain, then purée and cool.

Spread apricot mixture over the cooled shortbread. Beat egg whites with sweetener or sugar to taste, until stiff peaks form. Spread over the apricots, then return slice to the oven for 5 minutes, or until golden. Cool, then cut into fingers or squares.

Chocolate icing

2 cups icing sugar

4 tablespoons cocoa

2 teaspoons melted butter

Sift icing sugar and cocoa into a bowl. Add melted butter to 3–4 tablespoons warm water, then stir enough of the liquid into the sugar mix to make a spreading consistency.

Chocolate butter icing

60 g dark cooking chocolate, chopped

125 g softened butter

2 cups icing sugar

1–2 tablespoons warm milk

Melt chocolate in a double boiler over simmering water or on MEDIUM in the microwave. Set aside to cool.

Cream the butter, then gradually add sifted icing sugar alternately with milk, until soft and creamy. Beat in cooled melted chocolate until smooth.

Lemon or orange icing

1 teaspoon softened butter

2 cups icing sugar

2 tablespoons freshly squeezed lemon or orange juice

Beat together butter and sifted icing sugar. Gradually add the juice to achieve a spreading consistency.

Plain icing

2 cups icing sugar
2–3 tablespoons water or milk

Sift icing sugar into a bowl and gradually add enough water or milk to achieve a spreading consistency.

Vanilla icing

2 teaspoons softened butter
2 cups icing sugar
½ teaspoon vanilla essence
2–3 tablespoons water or milk

Beat together butter and sifted icing sugar, add vanilla, then gradually add enough water or milk to achieve a spreading consistency.

Conversions

(All conversions are approximate)

Oven temperatures

°C (Celsius)	°F (Fahrenheit)
150	300
160	320
170	340
175	350
180	355
190	375
200	390

Tin measures

cm (centimetres)	in (inches)
5	2
8	3
15	6
18	7
20	8
23	9
25	10
28	11
30	12
33	13
36	14
38	15
40	16
54	21

Weights

g (grams)	oz (ounces)
30	1
55–60	2
70	2½
85	3
100	3½
110	4
125	4½
140–50	5
170	6
200	7
230	8
250	9
285	10
340	12
375	13
450	16 (1 lb)
500	1lb 1½ oz

Liquid measures

ml (millilitres)	fl oz (fluid ounces – UK)
50	1¾
200	7
300	10½
600	1 pt 1 fl oz
1000 (1 litre)	1 pt 15 fl oz

Index

PENGUIN BOOKS

Published by the Penguin Group
Penguin Group (Australia)
250 Camberwell Road, Camberwell, Victoria 3124, Australia
(a division of Pearson Australia Group Pty Ltd)

New York   Toronto   London   Dublin   New Delhi   Auckland   Johannesburg

Penguin Books Ltd, Registered Offices: 80 Strand, London, WC2R 0RL, England

First published by Penguin Group (Australia) in association with the Country Women's
Association of Australia, 2009

10 9 8 7 6 5 4 3 2

Text and cover design by Claire Tice & Marley Flory © Penguin Group (Australia), 2009
Photography by Julie Renouf
Food styling by Lee Blaylock
Typeset in Avenir by Post Pre-press Group, Brisbane, Queensland
Scanning and separations by Splitting Image P/L, Clayton, Victoria
Printed in China by Everbest Printing Co. Ltd

National Library of Australia
Cataloguing-in-Publication data:

Country Women's Association biscuits and slices.
ISBN: 978 0 14 320232 5 (pbk.).
Includes index.
Biscuits.
Cookery.
Other Authors/Contributors:
Country Women's Association of Australia

641.5

penguin.com.au